Preacher

Preacher

The Wit and Wisdom of Reverend Will B. Dunn

by Doug Marlette

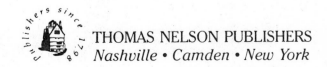

Publishers since 1798

THOMAS NELSON PUBLISHERS
Nashville • Camden • New York

Second printing

Published in Nashville, Tennessee, by Thomas Nelson,
Inc. and distributed in Canada by Lawson Falle, Ltd.,
Cambridge, Ontario.

Printed in the United States of America.
ISBN 0-8407-5895-2

To

Melinda

REVEREND DUNN, I'VE ASKED YOU HERE TO SEE IF YOU'D CONSIDER WRITING AN ADVICE COLUMN FOR THE "BUGLE."

BYPASS BUGLE

EDITOR

..AFTER ALL, YOU ARE AN EXPERT IN HUMAN RELATIONS!...

BUT... BUT I'M JUST A SIMPLE COUNTRY PREACHER! WHAT DO I KNOW ABOUT THE MEDIA?

MARLETTE

YOU'RE TOO MODEST, REVEREND... WHAT WOULD IT TAKE TO PERSUADE YOU TO DO IT?...

BYPASS BUGLE

EDITOR

TEN CENTS PER WORD, EIGHT INCHES ON THE LOCAL FRONT, TWELVE-POINT BOLD-FACE BYLINE, PAGE ONE PROMO AND PLAY ABOVE THE FOLD!...

BYPASS BUGLE

EDITOR

DID YOU DECIDE TO DO THAT ADVICE COLUMN FOR THE "BUGLE", PREACHER?

WELL, NOW, SON, THAT'S REALLY NOT MY CALLIN'...

BUT YOU SHOULD, PREACHER! REALLY!... YOU'D BE WONDERFUL!

AW, HUSH...

MARLETTE

C'MON, PREACHER, YOU SHOULDN'T HIDE YOUR LIGHT UNDER A BUSHEL! GO AHEAD AND WRITE IT!...

OH, I DUNNO...

"PEARLS FROM THE PULPIT!"

Dear Preacher,
I was fired from
my job.

My wife ran off
with my best
friend. My mother
contracted bubonic
plague.

My father is in
prison. I have
nowhere else to
turn. What can
I do?
          Desperate

Dear Desperate,
Whine,
Whine,
Whine!

Dear Preacher,
Modern life is
so impersonal.

All I want is to
be treated like
an individual.

In fact, don't reply
to my letter in the
newspaper. I prefer
a personal response.
          Unique

Dear Occupant,

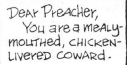

SON, I'VE DECIDED TO **SPECIALIZE**!...DOCTORS DO IT— WHY NOT MINISTERS?!...

SPECIALIZE? YOU MEAN YOU'LL NARROW YOUR MINISTRY TO A PARTICULAR AREA, LIKE VISITING THE SICK AND BED-RIDDEN?

NO WAY!

I DON'T MAKE HOUSE CALLS!

YESSIR, I'M GONNA SPECIALIZE MY MINISTRY!... A PREACHER OF MY GIFTS SHOULDN'T SPREAD HIMSELF TOO THIN!...

I'VE DECIDED TO LIMIT MY PASTORAL CARE TO A SELECT REMNANT OF THE SPIRITUALLY BEREFT!...

LIKE WHO?... THE POOR?... THE SICK?... WIDOWS AND ORPHANS?...

THE FABULOUSLY WELL-TO-DO.

MARLETTE

YESSIRREE!... CORPORATE LAWYERS, BUSINESS MAGNATES, ROCK STARS! WHEREVER THERE IS WEALTH AND PRIVILEGE, THERE, TOO, YOU'LL FIND THE REVEREND WILL B. DUNN!...

GOLLY!

FROM THE MANSIONS TO THE LEAR JETS, I WILL MINISTER TO THEIR EVERY NEED!...

WHAT NEEDS?

NOBODY LIKES A SMART ALECK, BOY!

MARLETTE

PREACHER, HOW DID YOU DECIDE TO MINISTER TO THE FABULOUSLY WELL-TO-DO?... YOU MUST'VE GIVEN IT A LOT OF PRAYERFUL CONSIDERATION...

I RECKON THE IDEA CAME TO YOU IN A FLASH OF SPIRITUAL INSIGHT AFTER DAYS AND DAYS OF AGONIZIN' SOUL-SEARCHIN'!...

MARLETTE

...OR WERE YOU FASTIN'?...OR MAYBE MEDITATIN' WHEN YOU FELT THE CALL TO MINISTER TO THE CULTURALLY ADVANTAGED?...

ACTUALLY, I WAS TAKIN' TEA WITH THE TADSWORTHS IN THEIR HOT TUB!...

.. NOW, I DON'T LIKE TO POINT FINGERS...

..BUT I WOULD HATE TO THINK THAT ANY MEMBERS OF MY CONGREGATION HARBOR HIDDEN RESENTMENTS OR PREJUDICE AGAINST THE MATERIALLY BLESSED...

REMEMBER—THE PRIVILEGED ARE PEOPLE, TOO!

NOW, NEXT SUNDAY I WANT TO SEE THIS SANCTUARY OVERFLOWING WITH THE RICH, THE ADVANTAGED AND THE WELL-HEELED FROM EVERY WALK OF LIFE!

ARE THERE ANY QUESTIONS?...

GOOD— IF NOT, WE'LL TURN TO PAGE NINETY-SIX IN OUR HYMNALS...

Dear Preacher,
I have fears too numerous to mention. I am afraid of everything.

This is excruciatingly painful. I need someone who will counsel me with sensitivity and understanding.

Can you help?
Frightened

Dear Scaredy Cat,

Dear Preacher,
Your column sounds like it is written by a seven year old.

Your advice is childish and immature. Why don't you grow up?!
A Reader

Dear Reader,
Liar, Liar, Pants on fire!

DEAR PREACHER,
I KNOW YOU'LL
UNDERSTAND.

I LIKE TO dress
up my microwave
IN WOMEN'S
Lingerie.

AM I NORMAL?

WONDERING

Dear Wondering,
What makes
you think I'll
understand?!

Dear Preacher,
My twin sister and I
think you are a phony.

There are enough so-called
"experts" making a fast buck
off of other people's problems
without you sticking your
big nose in where it doesn't belong!
What do you say to that?

MARLETTE

Dear Abby,

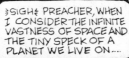

BEIN' A MINISTER MUST BE REALLY HARD, HUH, PREACHER?!

I MEAN, LIVING FOR OTHERS, LEADING AN EXEMPLARY LIFE! THAT'S A LOT OF RESPONSIBILITY! THE PRESSURES MUST BE TREMENDOUS!

HAVING TO SET A GOOD EXAMPLE!... PEOPLE WATCHING, WAITING FOR ONE FALSE MOVE, ONE SIGN OF HUMAN FRAILTY THEY CAN JUMP ON!... I DON'T KNOW HOW YOU HANDLE IT!...

I STAY HOME A LOT.

Y'KNOW, IN MY PROFESSION YOU HEAR A LOT ABOUT THE POOR AND DOWN-TRODDEN!... BUT, BY GOLLY, THE MATERIALLY BLESSED HAVE THEIR SPIRITUAL PROBLEMS, TOO!

THE FABULOUSLY WELL-TO-DO NEED MINISTERING TO AS MUCH AS ANYBODY ELSE!...

I RECKON.

IT'S A DIRTY JOB BUT SOMEBODY HAS TO DO IT!...

SURE, YOU'RE A VERY SUCCESSFUL BUSINESS TYCOON, BROTHER TADSWORTH, BUT ISN'T IT TROUBLING TO YOU WHEN YOU FORECLOSE ON WIDOWS AND ORPHANS?...

...ISN'T IT TROUBLING WHEN YOU CHEAT LOYAL EMPLOYEES?...

ISN'T IT TROUBLING WHEN YOU DOUBLECROSS FRIENDS AND BLACKMAIL COMPETITORS?!...

NO—WHAT'S TROUBLING ABOUT IT?

WHAT'S TROUBLING IS IT'S NOT TROUBLING!...

PREACHER DUNN, I LIKE YOU! YOU'RE MY KIND OF REVEREND! YOU KEEP YOUR MOUTH SHUT AND MIND YOUR OWN BUSINESS.

HOW WOULD YOU LIKE TO JOIN MRS. TADSWORTH AND ME AT THE CLUB FOR SUNDAY BRUNCH? SAY, ELEVEN O'CLOCK?...

WELL... OF COURSE, I HAVE MY SERVICE TO PREACH!...

CANCEL IT!

DON'T TELL ME, LORD!... LET ME GUESS!... THIS IS A TEST, RIGHT?

MARLETTE

Panel 1: ACTING AS YOUR ADVISOR IN MATTERS OF CONSCIENCE, SIR, IT HAS COME TO MY ATTENTION THAT YOU HOLD THE MORTGAGES ON THE HOMES OF SOME PENNILESS WIDOWS AND ORPHANS...

SO?...

MARLETTE

Panel 2: .. AND YOU'RE PLANNIN' ON FORECLOSIN' AND KICKIN' 'EM ALL OUT ON THE STREET FOR NO GOOD REASON!... AM I RIGHT?

WHAT OF IT?

Panel 3: OKAY... SEE... NOW THIS IS WHERE THE CONSCIENCE PART COMES IN!...

Panel 4: THE WAY I SEE IT, SIR, IF YOU KICK THOSE WIDOWS AND ORPHANS OUT ONTO THE STREETS, AT THE VERY LEAST YOU HAVE A P.R. PROBLEM!...

DADDY?

Panel 5: NOT NOW, VERANDA, HONEY... DADDY'S BUSY NOW...

I JUST WANNA SHOW YOU MY NEW CHEER!

MARLETTE

Panel 6: ROCKA-CHICKA-BOOM!... ROCKA-CHICKA-BOOM!... ROCKA-CHICKA-ROCKA-CHICKA-BOOM BOOM BOOM!

Panel 7: MIGHTY FINE, GIRL!... I'M PROUD OF YOU!

TEE-HEE!

Panel 8: NOW WHERE WERE WE?

WIDOWS AND ORPHANS.

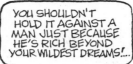

Dear Preacher,
I have trouble making a decision and sticking to it.

My friends and family are fed up with me.

Can I overcome my indecisiveness?
Wishy-washy

Dear Wishy-washy,
Maybe.
Maybe not.

Dear Preacher,
I am sick of these T.V. evangelists making millions off of their gullible viewers.

These "ministers" tell people to send them money and their problems will be solved. What can be done about these charlatans?
Disgusted

Dear Disgusted,
For solutions to these and other problems just send in a donation to me by check or money order c/o this newspaper.

Dear Preacher,
    Hey, you're a beautiful cat! No, I mean that sincerely....

You're a marvelous columnist and a great human being in your own right.
    Peace and Love

Dear Sammy Davis, Jr.,

Dear Preacher,
    Nobody treats me as an individual.

I feel like a nameless, faceless non-entity, undifferentiated from the mass of humanity.

I want to feel like a distinct human being with unique fingerprints and a specific identity. Any suggestions?
    Somebody

To whom it may concern,

UH-OH!.. MORE HATE MAIL....

Dear Alleged Human Being, You are a lousy little creep. I know where you live and I'm coming over to your house and punch you in the nose.

MARLETTE

THESE THREATENING LETTERS ARE ALWAYS THE SAME.... THE LITTLE COWARD PROBABLY DIDN'T EVEN SIGN HIS NAME!!...

Please find enclosed my name, address, social security number and references.

WITH HATE MAIL IT'S NOT SO MUCH WHAT PEOPLE SAY.....

T H O K

.... IT'S HOW THEY SAY IT!

MARLETTE

KNOCK KNOCK

ANOTHER LOST SHEEP SEEKING COUNSEL FOR DEALING WITH LIFE'S TRIALS AND TRIBULATIONS.

PREACHER, (SOB) I'M SO DEPRESSED!

WHAT IS IT, YOU POOR CHILD?!

I- I DON'T HAVE A THING TO WEAR TO THE TEA DANCE SATURDAY!

WE ALL HAVE OUR CROSSES TO BEAR.

YES, MA'AM!...YES, MA'AM!... I'M SORRY THE MISSIONARY SOCIETY IS UPSET, MIZ BARLOW....I FEEL JUST AWFUL ABOUT IT MYSELF....

...YES, MA'AM, I APOLOGIZE. ...I DON'T KNOW WHAT CAME OVER ME!...TELL THE BOARD OF DEACONS I'M REAL SORRY AND IT WON'T HAPPEN AGAIN! ...BYE, MIZ BARLOW!...

SIGH LIVE AND LEARN

CLICK

NEVER KEEP YOUR GOLDFISH IN THE BAPTISMAL POOL!

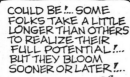

PREACHER, MAYBE MY PROBLEM IS THAT I'M A LATE BLOOMER!...

COULD BE!... SOME FOLKS TAKE A LITTLE LONGER THAN OTHERS TO REALIZE THEIR FULL POTENTIAL!... BUT THEY BLOOM SOONER OR LATER!...

REALLY, PREACHER?! DO YOU REALLY THINK I'LL BLOOM SOMEDAY?!...

'COURSE, IT'S ONLY A MATTER OF TIME BEFORE THEY FADE AND ROT!...

WHEN I'M FEELIN' LOW-DOWN AND POORLY, KUDZU, I LIKE TO READ THE STORY OF **JOB** AND HIS COUNTLESS HARDSHIPS, TRIALS AND TRIBULATIONS...

YOU MEAN YOU'RE UPLIFTED BY HIS EXAMPLE OF FAITH IN THE FACE OF UNENDURABLE SUFFERING?...

NAW — I JUST LIKE TO READ ABOUT FOLKS WORSE OFF THAN I AM!

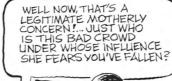

PREACHER, MY MAMA IS UPSET ABOUT YOU COUNSELIN' ME TO LEAVE HOME — BUT I KNOW IF YOU COULD JUST TALK TO HER ...

ANYTIME, SON — MY DOOR IS ALWAYS OPEN ...

GOOD — SHE'S WAITIN' RIGHT OUTSIDE!...

FUNNY — HE WAS HERE JUST A MINUTE AGO ...

WHY ME, LORD?...

OH, THERE HE IS UNDER THE LAMP-SHADE! (HE'S SUCH A CARD!)

PREACHER, THIS IS MY MAMA!

MIZ DUBOSE! SO VERY GLAD TO MEET YOU!...

YOU MISERABLE LITTLE VARMINT!

MAMA HAS A BONE TO PICK ...

WHY, MIZ DUBOSE, SO HAPPY TO FINALLY MEET YOU!... I CAN CERTAINLY SEE WHERE YOUNG KUDZU GOT HIS CHARM AND GOOD LOOKS!...

WHY, I DECLARE, REVEREND, HOW YOU GO ON!...

HEH-HEH, YOU SILVER-TONGUED DEVIL, YOU'VE STILL GOT IT!...

BUT YOU CAN FORGET THE LUBE JOB, SHORTY!...

WHERE DO YOU COME OFF ADVISIN' MY BOY TO DESERT HIS MOTHER?...

STAY CALM!... REMEMBER—SHE'S ON YOUR TURF!...

WHY, I COULD HAVE YOU UP BEFORE THE MINISTERIAL ASSOCIATION FOR MALPRACTICE!...

DON'T BE INTIMIDATED!... THEY CAN SENSE FEAR!...

PUTTIN' CRAZY IDEAS INTO THE HEADS OF IMPRESSIONABLE YOUTHS! YOU SHOULD BE ASHAMED OF YOURSELF!

BE GRACIOUS... HOSPITABLE... TAKE THE INITIATIVE!...

AND YOU CALL YOURSELF A MAN OF THE CLOTH!

CARE FOR A CHAW?

Dear Preacher,
I feel totally
alienated from other
people....

....and that nobody
is able to under-
stand me or empathize
with my feelings....

....Do you know what
I mean?

Estranged

Dear Estranged,
No.

Dear Preacher,
I can't stop
crying. I guess I'm
just a very sensitive
person but I weep
over anything.

I take everything
personally— a harsh
word, a rude gesture.
Please help me.

I need sympathetic
understanding from a
sensitive counselor
who will gently help
me overcome this problem.
That's why I'm writing
to you.
        Choked Up

Dear Crybaby.

Dear Preacher,
I am mortgaged to the hilt. I owe thousands of dollars in gambling debts.

The mob is after me. My wife is threatening to leave me. My own brother has sworn out a warrant for my arrest.

The bank is repossessing my car. You're my last resort.
Worried

Dear Worried,
Boy, am I glad I'm not in your shoes!

Dear Preacher,
I have a tendency to over-react to things. I make mountains out of mole-hills.

Is there any solution to my problem?
Hysterical

Dear Hysterical,
Simple. Change your name, get plastic surgery and move to Tahiti.

MARLETTE

PREACHER, BEFORE HE RAN OFF, WOULD YOU SAY MY DADDY WAS WELL-REGARDED IN THE COMMUNITY?

Words cannot express the esteem with which my father was held in the community.

MARLETTE

LIFE IS ROUGH, BOY, AND IF A MAN'S GONNA HACK IT HE'S GOTTA HAVE GUTS, STAMINA, DETERMINATION!...

I'VE GOT GUTS, PREACHER! I'VE GOT STAMINA!... I'VE GOT DETERMINATION!

MARLETTE

HE'S ALSO GOT TO BE IN TOUCH WITH REALITY.

PREACHER, MY PROBLEM IS PEOPLE!... I JUST DON'T GET ALONG WITH PEOPLE! IN FACT, I'D BE FINE IF I DIDN'T HAVE TO RELATE TO OTHER PEOPLE AT ALL!

MY BOY, A VERY WISE SUPERSTAR ONCE SAID, AND I QUOTE: "PEOPLE... PEOPLE WHO NEED PEOPLE... ARE THE LUCKIEST PEOPLE IN THE WORLD."

WHAT DOES THAT MEAN?

YOU'RE OUT OF LUCK!

I'M DESPERATE, PREACHER!... TELL ME, PLEASE!... WHAT IS THE MEANING OF LIFE?!...

PIECE O' CAKE, BOY!

LIFE (noun): THAT STATE OF AN ANIMAL OR A PLANT IN WHICH ITS ORGANS ARE CAPABLE OF PERFORMING THEIR FUNCTIONS OR IN WHICH THE PERFORMANCE OF FUNCTIONS HAS NOT PERMANENTLY CEASED.

THAT'S THE MEANING OF "LIFE."

THANK YOU, PREACHER.

HUMAN RELATIONS IS MY BUSINESS.

MARLETTE